TIMELINES

1930s

by
Gail B. Stewart

CRESTWOOD HOUSE

New York

Library of Congress Cataloging In Publication Data
Stewart, Gail, 1949-
   1930s / by Gail B. Stewart.
   p. cm. — (Timelines)
   Includes index.
   Summary: History, trivia, and fun through photographs and articles present life
in the United States between 1930 and 1939.
   ISBN 0-89686-474-X
   1. United States—History—1933-1945—Juvenile literature. 2. United States—
History—1919-1933—Juvenile literature. 3. History, Modern—20th century—
Juvenile literature. [1. United States—History—1919-1933—Miscellanea. 2. United
States—History—1933-1945—Miscellanea.] I. Title. II. Title: Nineteen thirties. III.
Series: Timelines (New York, N.Y.)
E806.S797   1989   973.917—dc20   89-34405
                                                                CIP
                                                                AC

Photo credits
Cover: Turner Entertainment (Gone With the Wind): Vivien Leigh starred as Scarlett
   O'Hara in the 1939 movie *Gone With the Wind*
   ©1939 Selznick International Pictures, Inc. Ren. 1967 Metro-Goldwyn-Mayer Inc.
FPG International: 4, 6, 7, 15, 16, 21, 23, 24, 26 (bottom) 32, 34, 36, 41, 44
Wide World Photos: 9, 11, 13, 14, 19, 25, 26 (top), 27, 28, 29, 30, 33, 37, 38, 39, 42, 46 (right
   and left)
The Bettmann Archive: 18, 20
New York Public Library (Schomburg Center): 45

Macmillan Publishing Company
866 Third Avenue
New York, NY 10022
Collier Macmillan Canada, Inc.

CRESTWOOD HOUSE

Produced by Carnival Enterprises

Printed in the United States of America

First Edition

10   9   8   7   6   5   4   3   2   1

CONTENTS

INTRODUCTION

Some decades open with a bang. The 1930s began with a whimper. America, the "land of opportunity," now seemed to have no opportunity at all. This was the Great Depression.

It was a time of people waiting in lines to get free food from church charity groups. It was a time of starving children whose parents felt guilty because they couldn't feed them enough. Every nickel was precious. Those who couldn't pay the rent were thrown out into the street. Millions of people were homeless.

Yet this was also a time when the government sponsored many programs to help people. Although times had never been tougher, most people had not lost hope!

During the Depression, some unemployed workers sold apples on the city streets.

1930

IT REALLY HAPPENED

In a one-room schoolhouse in West Virginia, the teacher noticed a little girl was pale. The child, whose name was Maybeth, seemed confused and sleepy. She was trying to pay attention to the reading lesson, but her head drooped down onto her desk.

The teacher took her aside and asked her what was wrong. Maybeth didn't answer. Puzzled, the teacher continued with the lesson, but she kept her eye on Maybeth for the rest of the morning.

At lunchtime, the teacher noticed Maybeth was not eating. Because the school was in a poor mining town, the children didn't have good lunches. But they always had something—even if it was only some bread and watered-down coffee. But Maybeth just watched the others eat.

The teacher thought Maybeth had forgotten her lunch. She

Children line up to get free food at a grammar school in England, Arkansas. Parents who could not afford to feed their families relied on local schools to provide meals for their children.

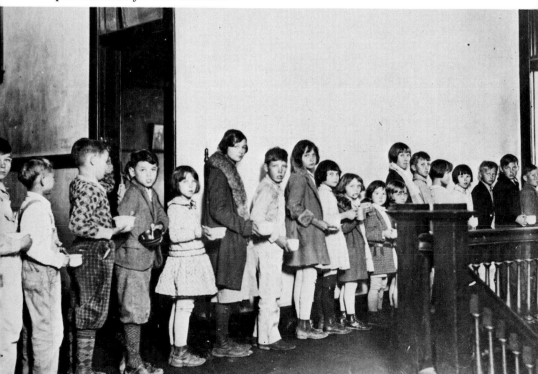

This migrant family in Texas could not afford a house or much food.

told Maybeth to go home and eat.

"No," said Maybeth. "It's not my day to eat. This is Tuesday —it's my little sister's turn."

Childhood was not carefree in those times.

BATTLE OF THE COLAS

In 1930, the Pepsi Cola Company was busy trying to compete with the Coca-Cola Company. Pepsi came out with a larger 12-ounce bottle. The cost was a nickel, the same price as Coke's 6-ounce bottle. The radio commercial for Pepsi said:

> *Pepsi Cola hits the spot,*
> *Twelve full ounces, that's a lot.*
> *Twice as much for a nickel, too.*
> *Pepsi Cola is the drink for you.*
> *Nickel, nickel, nickel, nickel,*
> *Trickle, trickle, trickle, trickle.*

1930

BACKING ACROSS AMERICA

In 1930, two friends decided it would be fun to drive across the United States backwards. Charles Creighton and Jim Hargis put headlights on the back of their Ford. They started their journey in New York.

The car's transmission was locked in reverse. The two men never drove faster than 14 miles per hour. It took them 42 days to get to Los Angeles, turn around, and come back to New York.

AMERICAN WINS NOBEL PRIZE

For the first time, an American won the Nobel Prize for literature. Sinclair Lewis was awarded the prize for his novel *Babbitt.*

EVERYBODY'S FAVORITE COOKIE

According to a recent survey, the Toll House (or chocolate chip) cookie is by far the most popular cookie in America. Many people don't know that the cookie was invented by accident.

A woman named Ruth Wakefield owned the Toll House Inn in Whitman, Massachusetts. (The inn got its name from the tollgate nearby.) Wakefield liked to prepare interesting and nutritious meals for her guests. She was especially fond of baking.

One day she planned to make chocolate cookies, but didn't have any cocoa in the house. Seeing a Nestle's Semi-Sweet Chocolate Bar in the cupboard, she decided to cut off little bits of that. The pieces would melt, she thought, and make good chocolate cookies.

The pieces didn't melt as she had predicted. The cookies Ruth Wakefield baked were a surprise, but a good one! The guests at the inn loved them. Word about the cookies spread. The Nestle Company made a deal with Ruth—they would give her a lifetime supply of free chocolate if she'd let them print her recipe

8

on the candy wrappers! She agreed, and soon everybody was making—and eating—Toll House cookies.

FAR-OFF PLANET PHOTOGRAPHED

Since the early 1900s, astronomers had calculated that a planet existed beyond Neptune. But it wasn't until March 1930 that they identified the planet Pluto by a photograph.

The extraordinary picture was taken at the Lowell Observatory in Flagstaff, Arizona.

The arrows point to the planet Pluto, discovered when it was photographed, for the first time, through a 24-inch telescope.

DRACULA COMING SOON!

In February 1931, Hollywood announced that a new movie would soon be released. The film was called *Dracula*. It promised to be a real spine-chiller.

The title role was supposed to have been played by Lon Chaney. However, Chaney died suddenly a few months before the movie was to begin shooting. The movie studio hired an unknown actor named Bela Lugosi to take Chaney's place. Lugosi's vampire became world famous.

KNUTE ROCKNE KILLED IN AIR CRASH

Knute Rockne was a football coaching legend. He was responsible for making Notre Dame into a football dynasty in the 1920s. The "Fighting Irish," as the team was known, became almost unbeatable under Rockne.

Rockne, along with seven others, was killed on March 31, 1931, in an airplane crash. The small plane was taking him to Hollywood, where he was to make a movie.

TALLEST BUILDING IN THE WORLD

Even though America was in the middle of a depression, work was completed on the Empire State Building. The skyscraper, located on Fifth Avenue and 34th Street in New York City, was expensive to build. Even so, owners wanted to feel hopeful about the future. They decided to finish the building as planned.

Towering 1,250 feet tall and containing 86 stories of office space, the building was an instant attraction. New Yorkers and visitors alike lined up for a tour of the building. The tour cost one dollar, which was a lot of money in 1931. But no one seemed to mind. "It is a bit of history we're seeing," remarked one man who stood almost two hours in line for the tour.

The Empire State Building as it looked in September 1930. The building was completed in 1931.

1931

CAPONE SENTENCED TO PRISON

"Scarface" Al Capone had committed many crimes in the 1920s. He had illegally sold liquor during Prohibition. He supposedly had ordered many murders, including the 1929 St. Valentine's Day Massacre in Chicago.

But it was not murder or bootlegging that put Capone behind bars in 1931. Instead it was tax evasion—not paying his income taxes! He was sentenced to 11 years in prison.

PLOP, PLOP, FIZZ, FIZZ

Hub Beardsley was visiting a friend in the local newspaper office of Elkhart, Indiana. Everyone was battling flu and colds, except the newspaper staff. Beardsley asked his friend about it.

His friend knew the reason. The editor of the paper gave a dose of homemade medicine to any employee who was coming down with a cold. The medicine was a combination of aspirin and baking soda. If taken at the first sign of a cold, it seemed to help.

Realizing how useful it could be, Beardsley rushed back to work and got chemists to create more of the remarkable medicine. They decided to manufacture it in the form of a tablet. This would be an easy, convenient way to take the medicine. Just drop a tablet in a glass of water, and wait for the results!

Alka-Seltzer, as the new drug was called, went on the market in 1931. It has been helping people feel better ever since.

THE ANTHEM IS OFFICIAL

On March 3, President Herbert Hoover signed an act that made "The Star-Spangled Banner" our national anthem. The words were written by Francis Scott Key in 1814. The anthem had been used in ceremonies for years, but it wasn't until 1931 that it was official.

Thomas A. Edison in his New Jersey laboratory

THE WIZARD OF MENLO PARK

Thomas Edison died on October 18, 1931, at the age of 84. Edison was nicknamed "The Wizard of Menlo Park," because more than 1,000 inventions came out of his laboratory in Menlo Park, New Jersey.

Edison was probably the greatest inventor America had ever known. Among his many inventions were the electric light, the phonograph, and the motion picture.

1931

A SHOCKING CRIME

Perhaps no crime is as horrifying to parents as the kidnapping of their child. Not knowing if the child is hurt or dead is a terrible feeling. But those were the emotions the national hero Charles Lindbergh and his wife felt in March 1932. While they were eating dinner, someone kidnapped their first child, 20-month-old Charles, Jr.

Leaning a ladder against the side of the house, the kidnapper climbed to the second-floor nursery where the baby was sleeping. In the little boy's room, he left muddy footprints and a ransom note. The note demanded $50,000 from Lindbergh, the first American to fly solo across the Atlantic.

More than 5,000 FBI agents as well as 100,000 police and volunteers searched for the child. Everyone hoped some clue would lead to the capture of the kidnapper and the safe return of the Lindbergh baby.

Tragically, that didn't happen. Two months later, the baby's body was found in the woods near the Lindbergh home. He had been brutally murdered, detectives said.

Left: Charles Lindbergh, Jr. Right: Charles and Ann Lindbergh and their three-year-old son Jon arrive in Liverpool, England, three years after the kidnapping. They had decided to leave the United States.

Unemployed men find food and shelter in a New York City church.

Bruno Hauptmann, a convicted criminal from Germany, was later charged with kidnapping and killing the baby. The evidence against him was powerful. He owned the ladder used in the kidnapping and had some of the ransom money. He was executed four years later.

HUNGRY AMERICANS

On September 12, 1932, a large crowd gathered in Toledo, Ohio. The people in the crowd were unemployed, frustrated, and poor. They were also angry because the government had cut off emergency relief to the unemployed.

The crowd marched into a Toledo grocery store and took as much food as they could grab. City officials said they felt sorry for the people, but taking food without paying was against the law. "It's a bad time we live in," said one council member. "Everyone is edgy and nearing the breaking point. To them, a loaf of bread is a precious treasure."

Monopoly was invented in 1932.

DO NOT PASS GO, DO NOT COLLECT $200

Monopoly, one of the two biggest-selling games in history, was invented in 1932. (The other biggest-selling game is Scrabble.)

In 1932, Charles B. Darrow, like many other Americans, was unemployed. He was a smart man who enjoyed games. Since he

16

had lots of time on his hands, he toyed with different types of board games. Since money was such a rare thing in the Depression, Darrow liked the idea of wheeling and dealing for lots of cash.

The game reflected the problems of the Depression, too. With one unlucky throw of the dice, a person could lose everything. To make the titles of the properties in the game interesting, he borrowed the names of streets from Atlantic City, New Jersey, where he had vacationed some years before.

The next year he took his game to Parker Brothers, who found it dull. They thought the rules were too complicated. But Darrow wouldn't give up. He borrowed money and had 5,000 of the games made up. He convinced a department store to stock Monopoly and was amazed at the response. The games sold immediately. People asked for more!

Parker Brothers, on hearing this, rethought their position. Perhaps the game wasn't too dull or complicated after all. They agreed to sell it, and Darrow became a millionaire. Today the game is played in 28 countries and has been translated into 19 different languages!

SPRAY-ON WHIPPED CREAM

When you think of ice cream sundaes, you probably take for granted that there will be whipped cream, nuts, and maybe a cherry on top. But until 1932, whipped cream wasn't used much in soda fountains. The reason was that whipped cream was hard to make. Every day a batch of the stuff had to be whipped by hand.

In 1932, Charles Goetz figured out how to change all that. Goetz was a chemistry major at the University of Illinois. He discovered that when he added "laughing gas" (nitrous oxide) to a canister of whipped cream, it could be sprayed! The same idea, he found, could also be applied to shaving cream.

NEW PRESIDENT IS OPTIMISTIC

On March 4, 1933, a new president took office. He was Franklin Delano Roosevelt (FDR), a Democrat from New York. He had had no difficulty in defeating President Herbert Hoover. People blamed Hoover for not leading America out of the Depression and back to prosperity.

When Roosevelt took office, more than 13 million people were out of work. Many families had been thrown out of their homes and apartments because they couldn't pay for them. They were living in shacks made of tar paper. They were looking through garbage dumps for food and clothing for their families.

Roosevelt gave a speech after his inauguration. He promised an end to financial troubles. He vowed that he would do everything in his power to put people back to work. In the most famous part of his speech, Roosevelt said, "The only thing we have to fear is fear itself."

President Herbert Hoover (left) rides with President-elect Franklin Roosevelt to the Capitol for Roosevelt's inauguration.

DY-DEE-DOLL

A new kind of doll came on the market in 1933. Called the Dy-Dee-Doll, it could "drink" a bottle of water and then wet itself.

NESSIE MAKES AN APPEARANCE

People have claimed to have seen a creature in Loch Ness, a deep lake in Scotland, since A.D. 565. The creature, known as the Loch Ness Monster, has been described in a number of ways: a giant frog, a dinosaur, and a huge snake with a tiny head.

The size of "Nessie," as it is also called, has been estimated at anywhere from 15 to 35 feet. Some say it has large humps on its back. It is said to be an air-breathing animal. There have been more than 10,000 sightings, some more reliable than others.

In 1933, a couple walking along a road near the lake reported seeing Nessie ambling across the road to the water. They said the creature was like a snail and had a neck longer than that of a giraffe. They watched Nessie for a few minutes and then reported the incident to their local paper.

This photograph, which claims to show the shape of the Loch Ness Monster, was taken in 1961.

Fay Wray starred with King Kong in the 1933 movie.

KING KONG SMALLER THAN HE LOOKS!

The first King Kong movie was made in 1933. The giant ape-like monster looked huge on screen. But the makers of the film said his size was an illusion. In each scene where King Kong appeared, the special effects crew either used a model made of clay or a hand puppet that was about 18 inches tall!

A "PURE" RACE?

In July 1933, Adolf Hitler announced that he wanted the German race to stay pure. He declared that everyone with an abnormality or deformity had to be sterilized. In other words, they would be operated on so they could never have children.

Those affected by this new policy included people who were blind, deaf, and disabled. Even though he wanted to deny many people their basic rights and even their lives, Hitler kept getting more and more popular.

FIRST COMIC BOOK

The first comic book was printed in 1933 but wasn't sold to the public. It was given out as a special gift by the Procter and Gamble Company and Canada Dry.

The comic was called *Funnies on Parade*. It was printed in four colors and contained several of the popular comic characters of the time—Joe Palooka, Mutt and Jeff, and figures from "Keeping up with the Joneses."

EINSTEIN COMES TO AMERICA

Albert Einstein, the greatest genius of our time, left his home in Germany.

Einstein, who was Jewish, left when Adolf Hitler came to power. In 1933, Hitler began making anti-Semitic speeches, calling Jews "the enemy of the German people." Einstein settled in Princeton, New Jersey, where he continued his scientific work in safety and peace.

Einstein had become famous as a theorist (a scientist who suggests ideas about hard-to-prove things). His theory of relativity was so complicated that even professional scientists couldn't understand it. But his ideas have held up. They have changed the way scientists think about time, space, gravity, and energy.

When Hitler came into power in Germany, Albert Einstein (third from right) fled to America to continue his work.

"WHEN I COULD GET AWAY WITH ONE"

Like other manufacturers, automaker Henry Ford got a lot of letters from customers. Some customers wrote how much they enjoyed the product. Others complained. But in 1934, Ford got a letter he would never forget.

The letter had been written by the famous gangster Clyde Barrow (half of the team of Bonnie and Clyde). Barrow wrote to say how much he enjoyed Fords.

"While I still have got breath in my lungs, I will tell you what a dandy car you make. I have drove [sic] Fords exclusively when I could get away with one."

A BELOVED CHILD STAR

In 1934, Shirley Temple was six years old and making $400,000 a year. That was an unbelievable sum during the Depression. How did she do it?

Shirley Temple was a movie star. She had dimples and curly blond hair. She could sing and dance and act remarkably well.

Most of all, she seemed to capture the public eye. In those days, the news was often gloomy and predicted more economic hardships. People were starved for happiness. Watching the little girl smile and sing her way through films was a welcome relief.

Shirley Temple made her first big movie, *Stand Up and Cheer,* in 1934. Although movies were a luxury for most families, people lined up outside theaters to see her!

GERMANY'S NEW PRESIDENT

In August 1934, Germany's president Paul von Hindenburg died. Adolf Hitler, the chancellor of Germany, stepped in to take his place. Although there was an election, most Germans were terrified of voting against Hitler—his power was already quite strong. Only 10 percent of the German people voted against him.

22   *Shirley Temple starred with James Dunn in the musical* Stand Up and Cheer.

Police finally found John Dillinger (in vest) in 1934, five months after he escaped from an Indiana prison.

PUBLIC ENEMY NUMBER ONE

John Dillinger was public enemy number one in 1934. He was a bank robber who stopped at nothing to avoid getting caught. A $25,000 reward waited for anyone who could help the FBI to capture him.

Dillinger had been in jail, but had managed to escape. The Indiana prison he was in was supposed to be "escape proof." But Dillinger whittled a piece of wood into the shape of a gun when no one was looking, and darkened it with black shoe polish. Then he waved the "gun" at the prison guards and forced them to let him out.

The prison staff was embarrassed at having been fooled by such a trick. But this was not the first time Dillinger had duped the police. He had also used many tricks to change his appearance. Every time a "Wanted" poster with his picture on it went up, it was immediately out-of-date. Dillinger had face-lifts, changed his hair color, and grew different styles of mustaches and beards. He even poured acid on the tips of his fingers to take away his fingerprints!

24

Maybe because he had fooled police so often, they were eager to catch him. In July 1934, they set up a stakeout outside a movie theater in Chicago. The FBI waited.

When Dillinger came out, he was shot and killed. Dillinger was accompanied by Anna Sage, a friend of Dillinger who told the FBI he would be there.

QUINTUPLETS!

In Ontario, Canada, five baby girls were born to Elzire and Oliva Dionne. Although other quintuplets had been born before, there was no record of all five surviving. The Dionne quintuplets were healthy and happy. They quickly became popular. People all over the world sent them cards and baby gifts.

Mr. Dionne with his five new baby girls

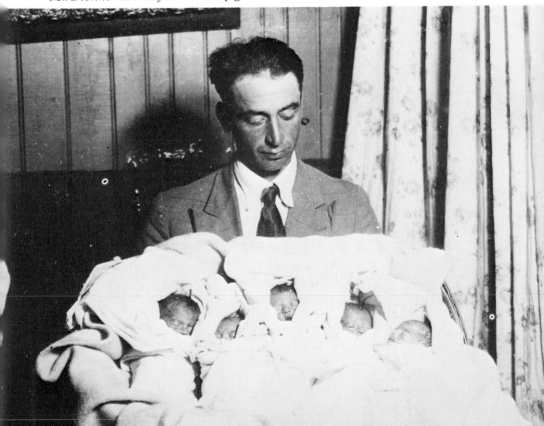

A huge dust cloud overcomes a ranch near Boise City, Oklahoma.

THE DUST BOWL

In 1935, the middle third of the United States was in terrible condition. Dust storms were raging over the Midwest, whirling away most of the good topsoil. Millions of dollars of crops were destroyed.

The storms seemed to go on and on. There was no relief in

A farmer near Garden City, Kansas, inspects the damage done to his tractor, buried in several feet of dust.

sight. Farmers who were already hurt by the Depression began to panic. Many just packed up and left their farms. Most headed west, where they assumed things would be better.

Those who stuck it out suffered. Blowing dust and dirt made the air so dark that lights had to be left on even during the day. The dust choked thousands of animals on farms.

The thick dust was harmful to humans, too. Many wore masks that filtered out the big particles, but even they didn't help much. Children and older people got pneumonia and other lung infections. The death rate increased. Life seemed to be put on hold as schools and businesses were shut down. Even funerals had to be postponed. The fierce storms made it impossible to bury the dead.

AN UNPOPULAR INVENTION

The first parking meters went into service in 1935. They were invented in 1933 by a man named Carlton Magee. He was the editor of a large newspaper in Oklahoma City, Oklahoma. He also served as head of the city traffic committee.

There were many cars in Oklahoma City by then, and parking was a real problem. No one knew what to do about it. It

Drought forced many Oklahoma families to leave their homes.

27

seemed wrong to keep building more and more parking lots. They were "a big waste of land," one businessman complained. So the task fell to Carlton Magee to devise a system that would control the parking in the city.

Magee's system turned out to be 150 meters. He placed them around the city. The people of Oklahoma City weren't thrilled at the idea of paying to park, but the city government loved it. The meters benefited the city in two ways. They cut down on the number of cars and they brought in money for the city!

300 MILES PER HOUR!

On the Bonneville Salt Flats in Utah, a new land speed record was set on September 3, 1935. Malcolm Campbell from England drove his sleek race car, the *Bluebird Special,* more than 300 miles per hour.

This amazing feat broke the old record, which Campbell had also set, of 272.109 miles per hour.

Sir Malcolm Campbell at the wheel of the Bluebird

Martin Luther King, Jr., who was not allowed to go to school with his white friends, is shown here speaking to a large crowd in 1967.

A HARD LESSON IN THE LIFE OF A GREAT MAN

Martin Luther King, Jr., was an important civil rights leader. King spent his life fighting hard for equal rights for black people. He believed that change should be nonviolent. Fighting, he said, would only cause more hatred and violence between black and white Americans.

Martin Luther King, Jr., had his first lesson in the hard ways of the world in 1935. He was only six years old.

That year, Martin had two best friends. They were brothers, and they were white. But color didn't seem important to any of the boys. All they knew about was playing and having fun.

That fall, the boys were ready to start school. But because they lived in Atlanta, Georgia, the boys would have to go to different schools. The law said blacks weren't allowed to go to white schools in the South.

King was sad at being separated from his friends. He was even more stunned when he went to his friends' house after school. The boys' mother told King that because he was a "negro," he was not to play with her sons. It was all right when they were pre-schoolers, but it didn't look right now that the boys were older.

29

The cover of
Life *Magazine's*
first issue

LIFE BEGINS

The first issue of one of the most successful magazines in history went on sale in November 1936. *Life* Magazine was different from other magazines of the day. Its emphasis was on pictures rather than words. The editors found that by searching for just the right camera shot or angle, a photograph could do as much, if not more, to tell a story.

Within six weeks of its first issue, *Life* had more than one million subscribers!

RUSSIAN COMPOSITION A CLASSIC!

Russian composer Sergei Prokofiev wrote *Peter and the Wolf* in 1936. It was an instant success around the world. Using music to tell a story was not new. But Prokofiev composed his music for young children. That hadn't been done often.

The story is about a young boy named Peter, whose grandfather warns him never to go into the forest. When Peter disobeys, it almost costs him his life.

Prokofiev uses a different instrument for each character. A narrator helps the orchestra tell their story. *Peter and the Wolf* is still one of the most popular children's compositions of all time.

A NEW BEST-SELLER

Until 1936, the top-selling book in America was *Uncle Tom's Cabin* by Harriet Beecher Stowe. But this year a new novel captured the lead. Within six months it broke sales records! The novel was Margaret Mitchell's *Gone With the Wind,* a romantic, exciting story set in the South during the Civil War.

BACK IN THE SADDLE AGAIN

During the day's fourth race at the Bay Meadows Racetrack in California, a young jockey named Ralph Neves was thrown from his horse. Horses and riders piled up, and a horse landed on top of Neves.

Medical personnel rushed out onto the track to help him, but it was too late. Neves had no pulse and no heartbeat. The 22,000 spectators at the racetrack were horrified. The public address speaker asked them to stand in silent prayer as Neves's body was taken to the morgue.

Less than an hour later, however, Neves woke up! He hadn't died. He'd gone into shock. But the jockey didn't know where he was. He didn't know why he was in a cold room wrapped in a white linen sheet.

He yelled, but no one heard him. Still clutching his sheet, he ran outside and persuaded a cab driver to take him back to Bay Meadows.

Everyone at the racetrack was astonished to see him. Doctors examined him and found nothing wrong with him. They gave the "dead" jockey permission to ride in the next day's races!

HITLER FOILED BY AMERICAN ATHLETE

The 1936 Olympic Games were held in Berlin, Germany. Adolf Hitler had hoped to use the games to show the superiority of German athletes over other "imperfect" races. He wanted to prove to the world that blacks, whom he considered inferior, couldn't beat white German athletes.

But Hitler was embarrassed by Jesse Owens, an American. Owens, a black man, won four gold medals. He won them in the 100- and 200-meter dashes, the running broad jump, and in the 400-meter relays.

Up until Owens's victories, Hitler had been personally congratulating the winning athletes in every event. Rather than shake Owens's hand, however, Hitler left the stadium. He told officials he was worried about rain, but no one was fooled.

Jesse Owens at the finish line during the 1936 Olympic Games

Jesse Owens receiving his gold medal from the president of the Olympic Committee. Broad-jumping winners from Germany (right) and Japan (third from right) flank Jesse Owens.

ELECTRIC BLANKETS NOW SAFE

The first electric blanket was invented in 1912. It was created to keep tuberculosis patients warm. Quite small, these first "blankets" were more like heating pads than blankets. They were also dangerous. More than one patient was burned or electrically shocked by poor wiring. Hospital staff had to monitor the blankets often to make sure the blankets were being used safely.

Many inventors tried to come up with a plan for a full-sized blanket. They wanted one that could be heated electrically and that was safe to use. In the 1920s one was made, but it cost $500! Few could afford it.

Finally, in 1936, technology made it possible to have a safe electric blanket. There was little danger of shock or fire. And the best part was that the blanket was affordable!

A SECOND TERM FOR FDR

After beating Republican Alf Landon, President Franklin Delano Roosevelt (FDR) won a second term. He was sworn in on January 20, 1937, a cold, rainy day. Roosevelt's advisors wanted him to ride inside a closed limousine because of the weather. But Roosevelt knew there were thousands of people lining the Washington streets hoping for a glimpse of him.

"No," he said, pointing to the crowds. "I'll ride in the open limo. If they can take it, I can!"

SNOW WHITE MAKES HER DEBUT

One of the most enjoyable full-length animated cartoons of all time debuted in 1937. Walt Disney's *Snow White and the Seven Dwarfs* was hailed by the public and the critics as a masterpiece.

The movie did have a bad side, however. The wicked witch, a scary old hag, was so frightening that many of the children in the

Snow White and the Seven Dwarfs *debuted in 1937.*

audience wet their pants! One theater reported that many of its velvet seats had to be reupholstered!

COOKING ON TV

January 21, 1937, was the first time anyone ever cooked on television. The cook was Marcel Boulestin. He demonstrated the proper way to prepare an omelette. The show, aired on the BBC in England, was the first of many cooking and baking shows to be on television.

NEW PLASTIC INVENTED

On February 16, 1937, the DuPont Laboratories announced that they had developed a new kind of plastic called nylon. Nylon, laboratory representatives said, was expected to be a very valuable substance in the years to come.

For one thing, nylon would replace silk in many cases. Women's stockings, which were made of silk, could now be made of nylon. They would sell for a fraction of the cost. The army was also interested in nylon for its parachutes.

The first commercial use of nylon came a couple of years later. Nylon was used in bristles for toothbrushes and hairbrushes!

TRAGEDY IN TEXAS

On March 18, a fire in a Texas school killed 500 people, most of them children. The fire began when a gas leak made the heating system explode. None of the children had a chance to escape.

Supplies and money from all over the nation poured into the Texas town of New London, where families had to deal with a horrible loss.

EARHART LOST AT SEA

World-famous flier Amelia Earhart and her navigator set out to fly around the world in 1937. They were somewhere over the Pacific Ocean when they vanished.

Two radio operators reported picking up faint signals from the plane, but they were unable to make out an exact location. Rescue operations were begun. But after several days the search was called off. Many Americans refused to believe Earhart was dead, however, and kept wishing for her safe return.

Amelia Earhart and Fred Noonan, her navigator, with a map showing the route of their last flight

FOOTPRINTS IN THE MOUNTAINS

In 1937, a photographer took pictures of some strange footprints. The prints were thought to be proof that a creature called the Abominable Snowman really did exist!

The Abominable Snowman, or "Yeti" as it is called in Tibet, has been a creature of legend for more than 300 years. More than 40 people claim to have seen the beast. They say it is stocky, tailless, and covered with hair. They also report that it has a huge mouth, a pointed head, and walks on two legs.

The Yeti supposedly lives in the towering Himalaya mountains of Asia. Many mountain climbers and explorers claim to have seen footprints. Some said they made contact with the beast. The footprints weren't "verified" until 1937. Since then, more sets of huge, mysterious footprints have been photographed. In 1972, plaster casts were made of some.

Is there such a thing as an Abominable Snowman? If not, what could be making such footprints? A huge bear? An ape? No one knows for sure!

Amelia Earhart

1938

IT'S A BIRD, IT'S A PLANE . . .

Superman, the one who could leap tall buildings in a single bound, came to life in 1938. That's when the very first Action Comic was published, telling the story of the boy from Krypton who came to Earth.

Collectors of comics would love to get their hands on that first issue. It cost only a dime in 1938. Today it is worth more than $18,000!

NOT A RECORD TO BE PROUD OF

The Chicago Bears had always been a good team. They had played in many championship football games. But in 1938, they achieved what no other football team had ever done. And, said one team member, the Bears hoped they never would get such an "honor" again. They fumbled more times that season than any other team in history—56 times!

The first Superman comic book

THE MARTIANS HAVE LANDED!

A radio broadcast set off panic all over the country on October 30, 1938. Orson Welles, a popular radio personality, directed the broadcast of H. G. Wells's *The War of the Worlds*.

The play was about Martians landing and causing the end of the world. The producers of the broadcast gave a warning at the beginning of the show. They told people that although it would sound "real," the events were just for fun. It was even discussed in the morning paper. But some people never got the message.

People ran through the streets of New York with handkerchiefs over their faces to protect themselves from Martian gas. Hundreds of others took to their cars. They drove out of the city to escape the aliens.

Although the radio play had some very realistic parts, no one thought it would result in such panic!

1938

After his radio broadcast of The War of the Worlds *sent many listeners into a panic, director Orson Welles met with reporters and said he was amazed the program had caused so much trouble.*

WRONG-WAY CORRIGAN

In 1938, a 31-year-old pilot named Douglas G. Corrigan decided to fly his plane from New York to California. Officials had denied him permission, however. His battered old plane had failed every safety inspection. The plane did not even have a radio.

But Corrigan was stubborn. He came to the airfield and told the mechanics there that he was bound for California. They watched him take off in the old plane, and then stared in amazement as he curved in the wrong direction.

For 24 hours he flew. He thought he was going west. He was really heading east toward Europe. There had been heavy fog, so it was impossible for him to see anything. He landed in Dublin, Ireland, and told air traffic officials there that he had accidentally gone the wrong way.

You might think that he would be punished for his mistake, or at least for disobeying orders. But he was hailed as a sort of hero! He was given a ticker tape parade in New York when he returned. Later a movie was made about "Wrong-Way" Corrigan.

A NEW KIND OF PLAY

In 1938 a play called *Our Town* opened in New York. Written by Thornton Wilder, the play was very different from what American theatergoers were used to seeing.

The play was performed without any scenery. "Imagine it for yourselves," the narrator told the audience. After all, it was about the audience's lives, too.

A NEW WAY OF WRITING

A Hungarian hypnotist named Lasalo Biro came up with a new way of writing in 1938. At the time, people were still using fountain pens and bottles of ink. Biro found a way to make ink dry quickly. He invented the modern ballpoint pen.

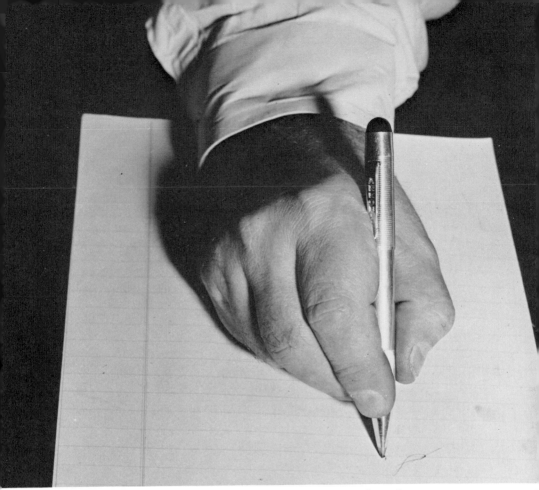

One of the first ballpoint pens being introduced at a National Hardware exhibit in New York City

CRYSTAL NIGHT

Angry emotion against Jews reached terrifying heights in Germany in 1938. On the night of November 9, young Nazi followers of Hitler stormed into the streets armed with hammers and rocks. They killed Jews and destroyed their synagogues and stores. There was so much broken glass in the streets that the night was afterwards called "Crystal Night." The memory of it is still a horror today.

1939

AND ALL FOR 25 CENTS

One of the hit movies of 1939 was *The Wizard of Oz*, starring young Judy Garland.

Did you know that in 1939, a kid could go to the theater, see a film, a cartoon, and a newsreel, and buy two large candy bars—all for a quarter?

NAZI GERMANY INVADES POLAND

Hitler's German army invaded Poland on September 1, 1939. More than one million German soldiers were aided in this attack by soldiers from Russia. (Hitler and Joseph Stalin, Russia's premier, had signed a treaty.) It took less than three weeks for Poland to fall.

World leaders condemned the attack. People everywhere worried about another world war.

"This is terribly wrong," said an American correspondent. "We've had only 21 years of peace following the war that was supposed to be the last war. It looks like certain danger on the horizon."

THE POWER OF THE PRESIDENT

Although it had never been done before, the date of Thanksgiving was officially changed for 1939. The holiday should have fallen on the last Thursday of the month—November 30. But Roosevelt announced that he was changing it to November 23, one week earlier. This would provide more space between Thanksgiving and Christmas, he explained. Abraham Lincoln had set the original date in 1864.

TOO VIOLENT

Dr. James Naismith, who invented the basketball in 1891, decided that the game had become too violent. Naismith had tried to invent a game that had none of the roughness of football, but was still active and fun.

But in 1939 Naismith went on record as saying modern rules had ruined the game. He hated the zone defense. He called it a "stalling tactic that leads to roughness."

He said, too, that the officials let players get away with too much elbowing and contact.

ROLLO, THE RED-NOSED REINDEER?

In 1939, the people at the Montgomery Ward store in Chicago wanted something special to give away to kids at Christmas. Usually a department store Santa gave out candy or some small treat. But this year, the store wanted something a little different.

Robert May, who worked in the store's advertising department, came up with a poem about a reindeer with a shiny nose. The reindeer helped Santa get the toys out on a foggy Christmas Eve. May's friend Denver Gillen, who was an artist, made colorful sketches to go along with the poem.

The problem was that they couldn't decide on a name for the reindeer. May had suggested Reginald or Rollo, but the store owners didn't like the sound of those.

A German motorcycle unit, followed by trucks, invading the town of Bromberg, Poland, in 1939

Finally, under pressure from his four-year-old daughter, May suggested "Rudolph." Everyone agreed. The illustrated poems about Rudolph, the Red-nosed Reindeer, were given out to children at the store.

It wasn't until 1947 that the poem was put to music. It became the second-best-selling record of all time!

A NATION OUT OF WORK

Despite efforts to turn the economy around, Roosevelt's administration announced in 1939 some grim statistics. There were 10 million people out of work. Children were starving. Many left home at age 10 or 11 to find odd jobs and earn a few pennies.

ELEANOR ROOSEVELT RESIGNS

In 1939, a young singer named Marian Anderson was invited to perform in Washington, DC. Anderson, a world-famous clas-

A homeless family packs all their belongings and travels the country looking for work.

The classical singer Marian Anderson (in front of piano) performs at the Lincoln Memorial.

sical singer, was to sing at Constitution Hall. But the plan hit a snag.

The Daughters of the American Revolution (D.A.R.) said that Anderson, a black woman, had no business performing at Constitution Hall. The D.A.R. is an organization of women who pride themselves on being descendants of the first white settlers in America.

Eleanor Roosevelt, the wife of the president, was angry about the D.A.R.'s decision. She, too, was a member of the organization. She promptly resigned.

Mrs. Roosevelt organized an alternate site for the concert—the Lincoln Memorial. She personally greeted the famous singer there. More than 75,000 people came to hear the concert.

INDEX

A German tank moves into Warsaw, Poland, which surrendered to the German army on September 27, 1939. When Germany invaded Poland, many people predicted the beginning of World War II.